ACQUAINTED

POEMS

ALISHA CHELSEA JONES

12/17/2019

To the fearless Dalrina. With boundless love, My heart to you.

—alisha jones

This publication contains the opinions and ideas of its author. It is intended
to provide helpful and informative material on the subjects addressed in the
publication. The author and publisher specifically disclaim all responsibility
for any liability, loss, or risk, personal or otherwise, which is incurred as a
consequence, directly or indirectly, of the use and application of any of the
contents of this book.

WRITERS REPUBLIC L.L.C.
515 Summit Ave. Unit R1
Union City, NJ 07087, USA

Website: *www.writersrepublic.com*
Hotline: *1-877-656-6838*
Email: *info@writersrepublic.com*

Ordering Information:
Quantity sales. Special discounts are available on quantity purchases by
corporations, associations, and others. For details, contact the publisher at
the address above.

Library of Congress Control Number: 2019951427
ISBN-13: 978-1-64620-081-8 [Paperback Edition]
978-1-64620-082-5 [Digital Edition]

Rev. date: 10/22/2019

The Disclaimer

This is a work of fiction. Names, characters, places, and incidents either are the product of the authors imagination or are used fictitiously and any resemblance to actual persons, living or dead, business establishments, events or locales are entirely coincidental.

Perfect coincidences enclosed.

Dedication

You know who you are.

Thank you for saving me.
Thank you for listening when you did not have time.
Thank you for loving this moment for me.
Even though time isn't real.

To my family, friends, and followers.

I love you.

I wrote this book for you.
I think we know each other?
I think you love me.
Right?
You might not know yourself yet.
That's the problem.
It's hard getting acquainted with exactly who You are.
    Let me help you
    in This Life.
I can show you how.
    I'll go first.

Preface

Let's get acquainted.

Promise me you will read for
    enjoyment
        not just dissection

I am all in here
my truth and vanity and grace and peelings and wrongs

are all in here

I tremored
    in
release

my hands sweat and
smeared ink again and again

for the release

I deleted everyone in my life
who took too much of my mental space

for the release

sat ugly in my house
    on Friday night
wept alone

for this release

I purged my old life
shed Skin to Gold

for this release

I shook uncontrollably

In anger
In guilt
In disappointment
In waiting
to be strong enough

    to release

I waited thirteen years for you to read

    Me

do not make me small
to make these readings
comfortable for you

I want you bothered
I want you to re-read these
    words
      and find six of the eighteen meanings

I want you to send photos of it to your friends
Because we are All in It
and its Raw.

Thank you for buying my book.

There's a nude in here too, enjoy.

I tell you all about the Others
the Makers of me
who molded my personality
and random encounters along the way

I tell you all about my Lovers
The favorable and the furious

But then I tell you the Rest

There has never been a more prolific way to start that
conversation
Of cryptically hiding in plain sight

…and then there's The Riddle, of course.

So go fucking read it
Through to the end
Comment on Instagram, I want to hear from you.

Forreal.

Art is exposure in the art of exposure.

This is my Truth.

The Realest Shit You've Ever Read.

Contents

To The Makers

Thank you
 To the
Makers

the few who started
then discarded

those who
ground their thumbs
to mold my flesh

strong

smoothed

the Artists
with paint and pity

stroked my rippled sides

flashed
kiln

beyond a long weeks work

thank you
to the material

the hurt of Polishing
crackled to shine of
a masterpiece encased

I am Made Art.

chiseled with fragility
furious and serene

I
Am
Art

We are artists.
Thank you to the Makers.

The Brief Passage

She threaded cement when her hands were steady
and gave us backbones
nursed us, hawked us
like ripe tomatoes
     when the storm came we would hang and wade
glisten when the clouds
 walked away
 like everyone else.

She raised us in a perfect anger
a natural vibrato laced my ears
her speech
burnt
orange refinements
layered meanings
that
caramelized character
like an aged black skillet

I am her crisp manifesto

writhing laborer with a stubborn sweetness
a sweating palm with a firm word
She lives here
buried
in my chest
feet deep in my conscious

She
        Moves.

rivets at my dishonesty
dances in success

Unmatched.

subtle Greatness
unknown fears

She's my old soul
vinyls
volumes that created breaks
She
lives
here
        In the free of Today

Can't miss her
        Gummy smile
Muted perfumes

Can't miss her

She's always Behind me.

Why I Hated Ohio

"Roofied"

Is drowning on air

I gasped
for what felt like
eternities
on the thick of Helpless

then Myself left me
        and He took my place
         My Places

My feminine

and the pain of it all
lurched forward
violence
vomit

Not a single one of my 10k followers could see

        me

No beauty
No glamour

I devalued
as the chipped paint and skin
under my fingernails
stripped
        In a littered bathroom

humiliation is
closing your eyes
          seeing pink
wishing

          for anything but Ripping
my clothes were ripped
my skin ripped
my voice ripped
All of Me was Ripping

into a dizzy silence

she never noticed
      I went missing.

dissolved out of my skin and flesh
sweat a Fear twisted to sickness
my brain protected my Soul

I disappeared.

He never noticed I went missing.

I do not know
who
has Me

As limp body hangs
the handicapped rails

I will never
know
his name
Of all
that hurts most

The Entering of Me with No Name.

I flailed
kicked
    fought
until I forgot where I Was.

I Wasn't.

being a Nothing
to someone's Needs

can make you hollow

taken
        left outside
    of body
of mind
Of the club

looking as a pauper
To any other stranger

Please Help Me.

"I need home."

hold my heads
I am Lost

I am sorrow
I mean
I am sorry

"Me?"

"Sorry,

shiver.

"I don't know
my Name."

billowy piano cords
at 2am in Chicago o Hare
    drew
A custodian sneaking notes
with hands only thought good for
Gloves and gathering

those notes matter

in the shiftless
miracle of just over midnight
palm morning over us

reminding us the mystery
of our dreams deferred
lay
    over
    walk me through
    your story
Its ok.
I'm fortunate in hearing
    you.
I can listen to your secrets.
I like our mystery.

take me further
keep playing

you dropped your magic
over the keys
lost found new tickets home

palm morning over us
flesh and cold coffee down the sink first
our mystery

Clink cold round sounds
Ear drums search new
feelings
surprise me
with hands only thought good
for gloves and gathering

Smooth them clatters
make me make a fool of myself
in this dancing
you caught me

those steps matter

reminding the mystery
of my dream Deferred
it hurts less when you start
    First
lay
   over
walk around my story

we witness what
we would
whisper about
at 2am in Chicago o Hare
We know there's more

Steps.
Scales.
secret.

I like our Mystery.

Two Day Hair Appointment (Slam)

I'm younger
Than my hair.
mine swings of ancient tribal freedom.

I coiled love into these coils
and they sat where I put them.
That makes you and I different.

It's not "exotic"

It's a pressing to an ancestor.

Don't let the colors fool you
We pride our hair
As Power Should

The braids are blackness
Pulled from the root
Of the root
To the Roots

We sway here
New and unchained

Regard Our Essence
We sip the Royalty
Out of your breeze

"How
    did
      you
    get
      your hair
like that?"

Get inquisitive, Karen.

We're more than thick thighs and cowrie shells.

There's art on my scalp
greased up the back
divinity down our front

We know sacrifice
It looks like it's painful because it is.
But it's worth it
edges get snatched
We count time
In the new section she started braiding
But it's worth it
My ass hurts sitting for 7 hours
But it's worth it
Tylenol over hair tyranny
No strenuous activities
They haven't loosened up yet
But it's worth it

5 bathroom breaks and a soda
A book maybe
I can't text with my head at this angle
To the heavens
It's so worth it
But I don't want to miss
This sacred ceremony
Of loving the Blackest part of me

It won't "hurt" after a few days

We
    know
Hurt.

We go without sometimes
And that brings us together
Raised fists in every shade

We don't weather the pain of braids for you, Richard.

We do this for Us.

We hold every yesterday
In each twist, each loc, each fade.

Protective styling for us
Is
Protecting our culture
from you

We were told it was "too ethnic for the workplace"

But fuck that. And fuck them. I just paid hundreds of dollars to

Glow
  like
    this.

Put that hair flip in slow motion video
For all of us.

A soft pat and an oiled scalp
Does it
For me.

You're going to stare.
Yes, get uncomfortable
asking me to change
A culture woven into me, Karen from
HR.

TRY
   ME
while my braids are fresh, bitch.

We hold space for our pain.
Of the fitting
   In
That you just can't understand.

We took your ropes
Freed our hair from your stories

Yes,
it may take two days.

It's freedom to us
Old and New

It will take two days on this journey

But it's the Union

Of us
To Home.

Plea to the Elocutionist

"Elocutionist- summon contentment to my ears
vexed below the murmur of soulless judgment
grace me with your demise
lose me in the depths of your diction..."

The wordsmith divulged my presence
as faultlessness exits his esophagus
audible calligraphy scrolled the atmosphere
from a grey inked decadence

"Elocutionist- caramelize the air
where floweth found perfection..."
spoken text spinning subjects
beneath crafted letters of excellence

"Loose your tongue to entangle my confidence..."

Resolve me here
in the riddle of your sentences
for I am the tempest error
lacing speeches predicament

"Elocutionist- Why may I splice your words of artistry?"

Free me as the flaw
from your spoken precision

To my Mom.

I put these words on paper
so you never forget

how

I felt

You.

the harm was that you were missing
your omission of action
was felt.

you trusted me to conquer the world
and I did

but you never
worried
about how I would do it
or how it would hurt
to do it by myself

You knew I would
figure
things
out

but you never cared
how

If it was scary
If I was making things harder than I needed to make them
If I bumped my head and bled out

If I cried.

I did.

I shed
scalding hot, thick tears
the kind you only get from
being left

Alone

and all the while knowing
I'll survive without you anyway
knowing you'd be proud
but waiting on a call
that never came

I needed
You
in the in-between

but I went anyway.

and for that I am stronger than you

so these words are here

to
tell you
to reach

Back
to Me.

I'm here, I still cry.
I will always be "the little one."

I love you.
I love you Mama.
I am proud of who you've become.
I forgive us.

but
know

I save myself

every fucking time.

By Consumption

The consistency of a dream
dripped
realities about my tea
and I
was to sip
an existence

the viscosity denied me
unfavorable plea
and keen
was I to drift
readily
gluttonous in the throat of imagination
one tamed a honeyed flavor
flowing lifetimes indulgence
within me
and I
a loyal customer
ingested the sweetened stupor
now poisoned
by appetite's decree

You should answer the phone.

Things haven't fallen into place. Its more like bed sheets- shifted and not quite where they should be. I feel that tug, that pull and tuck to make things move to where they're needed and I cannot rest comfortably without a settled place to lay my burdens.

I prayed today.

Its been a long night.
I've seen everyone who mattered, and passed those who didn't at a few red lights.
Nothing is farther from view than those "objects" that "appear closer."

I'm
done reflecting
on spite.

I want to dream. I haven't in a very long time.
I have gotten so used to nightmare that I look around the room for hours at all the monsters that may be lurking.
I find myself greeting them through email in the morning.

My professor asked me what family was.
I told him 2 or more people setting out to support and love one another and be involved in each other's further.
He replied "Family is in the eye of the beholder."

I've been squinting for a long time, too.

I love you all. I am so tired of trying to prove it.

I'm human. And when I realized that everyone else was too life began to make much more sense. I can't hold in my disgust or malice due to a lack of understanding.

I've always understood
but
I
never
wanted
to accept it, so

I'm sorry my existence let you down but
Today is the day I really just let it go...

And this apology goes to whoever I thought got in the way of my conclusion.
There are no coincidences.

You
told me
the truth

And all the Mishol's and Tarah's in the world have no idea how much I admire them, no matter what.

I missed God. And I thought maybe He was just taking a break
but He wasn't.
He was
breaking me in
so I could cover the corners
and dream of seeing humanity

I could be wrong
but it'd be more wrong not to tell someone

I am scared
And I'd never tell anyone I'm terrified beyond belief about the
"next steps"

all 1,838,578,584 of them.

I miss home
I miss my old world
and I miss my Love

but

I

woke up
Early
this morning.

The Patio Set

left outside
after moves

I grow less new
lumber
in the colder months
peeling
in Peace
seasoned and conquered
aged
tattered
    Learned.

be rusted
ash around the limbs
dusked with rain
antique by exposure
to Days without time
sun-dried and freed
I grow
    less new
but
    I
Grow

Baby Snatcher

I'm a beast, a mindless monster, a spineless Snake, boa
constrictor squeezing the life out of your perfect home,
that's
what they call us
child protective services workers

See we show up unannounced unapologetic
And we work 8 to 5 Monday through Friday but
Saturday at 2am
I slithered through the grass to her door with the broken locks
When she yelled through the window
"Fuck off, baby SoandSo isn't here"
But we didn't leave
we don't just leave

It's Saturday night, and I'm suppose to be wasted

But I stay because Baby SoandSo had some
nights,
some Saturday nights being wasted in the womb
And now Baby SoandSo is a little slow but showed up at school
with a black eye then disappeared for a few days
Truant with new bruise on top of old bruise
Or with someone making bruises we won't ever see
So no I'm not festering here for funsies, so open the door
I reply " No, Mrs. SoandSo, I need to speak with you and baby
SoAndSo right now."

Hiss hiss.

The moon charms me to the porch to see
Baby SoandSo's little black eye peeking through a window on
the other side
Because to him trash bags have always covered Windows
And the house
like his life has always sat crooked on its foundation
And he's always been made to say that he "fell off the couch"
when the bad things happen
to his body
When others ask
I'm a boa
I'm a constrictor
Squeezing through the door With cops
Hashing out lies with Mrs.SoandSo who told the same lies two
months ago,
But we didn't have enough to take it to court so we had to let
the whole case go
I'm choking a home
Sending junkies over the couch through the Backdoor

Taking babies out of carry-on suitcases

But all you heard was that I snatched a baby.

I'm a beast
A mindless monster
When Mrs.SoandSo says
"CPS can have it,
    I never wanted it anyway."

With my powerful jaw I swallow him whole like the innocent bird
that he is,
I only take
him
because
His clothes smell of urine and missed play dates
His welts are purple and teal, and grey
He doesn't even have a toothbrush
I only take
him
because
he's all that there is to take

It's Saturday night and
I'm not stealing someone's Uber
I'm dodging curse words and airborne car seats
Hiss hiss
He's the egg in my throat when I'm driving through the middle of
Nowhere to Somewhere Ranch Foster home,
the face that keeps me awake when we pull over to vomit,
the voice that brings tears to my eyes when he says,

After years of abuse,
after never learning to tie his shoes,
after growing up in closets and missing meals for weeks,

he says
"Miss Alisha, can I go home?"

And now
I'm a monster
to him too.

"She'll figure it out..." And other misplaced wishes. (Slam)

My rich friends from old money won't understand this poem.

but know

It's hard being upright
nobody asks twice about when you make mistakes
no one worries

when you have more than you used to.
not much more, but just enough.

inches to survive.

risks are calculated
succeed or be hungry
that divides us

the other pretty girls
don't know what I know
        well
We
make career survival
carnivorous business
diet wholesome
        we vacillate
between making sure "we got" everyone
even though we lucked out this month
on scratch-offs

I know that luck.

She's inconsistent
heats acid in belly

I'm nervous enough
we don't
have enough

may I be sad now?
I don't have time to feel anything.
I am
working double shifts
Can we share a ride or not?
text me faster so I don't miss this bus.

we keep going
a little while longer.

I'm drunk at Waffle House with nothing.
I'm not gonna dine and dash
but I thought about it
longer
than I would like to admit.

that broke that lives day to day
        where
the instant meals
need to stretch
        longer
than we would like to admit.

I'm stretched past this instances.

we do this to ourselves.
there's no one to catch you when
you fall.
I fall.
Family falls.
You're the catcher
Everyone is laying down already

It's not baggage
It's your brother's baby.
It's somebody's transmission
It's daycare. It's always fucking daycare.

we know we can take leaps forward
and never look back
but it never feels quite right
to lose humility

whenever the Don't Haves show up.
and everyone has to adjust

we don't forget those looks.

Going Without had a Face
like mine.
Going Through makes tired
set your bones.

you are asking me too many questions
at this rich bitch party.

I blush
ashamed of things far from
        my control

we didn't have cable to watch
        that
we didn't have cars that could make it that
            far out

my palette isn't sophisticated but
I know what sleep taste like.

Savings?
See I write jokes, too.

Do they want us?
I guess not all the time.

I knew better when they didn't know best.

the in-between times are
how we glean Grace
how we learn grit

no one worries
Survival is sanity
we tow the line
        to shreds
            We break
I'm broke
hauling cans of green beans up the hill

that pain stretches
    longer
than we would like to admit

Don't print the receipt
That's $2.06 fee is $2.06 too much
Now I'm at $17 and I can't take 20 out from anything.

ISF. My rich friends from old money don't even know what that
means.

A modest Sankofa
sees works from my backside
the nervous
heavy
that makes everything louder than
necessary

Swipe. Processing payment. Beep. Did it go?

are three meals "necessary"
we can go longer...

until our air snacks turn stale.
or were they like that when we bought them?

we do this to ourselves
we don't ask for help
or a ride
or a lunch
or to buy time to make more time to have more time to spend
more money we didn't have to begin with

plate clean
        mind clutters
I stuttered over
        questions
you didn't ask
when you're living upright

no one worries
we keep going
we make due

for a little bit longer.

Despite the declining balance
that tackles my itunes gift card
hardly am I trapped by soundlessness
I am forced to fixate my mind
on the idea that silence is
a penitentiary
and that music is free
and that
music
is
freedom

music is the soul of a man
music makes a happy day
music makes the clouds roll by baby
your music is the tears inside my
eyes

when the life on my back gets too heavy
and tomorrow gets too tough
and people who looked for guidance
got lost
losing music
would hallucinate me
to bend circumstances
around the circumferences
of bleak angles
angels
passed my many

silent nights
without a nativity scene
by singing
wise man to heaven
in hymnals because happiness
happiness today is just a song away,
its just
a song
just a jill scott run
just a fiasco flow
just another note
exfoliating every moment
in the flesh of my existence
and without it
I am that arrested development

Why?

because
I live
beneath treble-clefs
rested on the scalps
of bobbing heads
because my hair is hued hip-hop
roots
are nappy and kinked with reggae
atop the face that
sees sounds move nations
I'm complacent
 with the tapping of feet
 to the jazz quartet

or better yet
these arms
that strength round
to the motherland
and sway oppresses
in the atmosphere
of african beats
your seats should be empty
and you should be standing
there is music somewhere
playing
in this building
on his mind
on her lips
and in your heart

and damn it sounds good.

You don't have to be quiet
because music can fill every breath
you don't have to be scared
because music
notes
your every fear
you don't have to cry
because music
paints every shade of Blues

so when you wake
and break day
playing cassettes, disc or tape
remember
the headphones you spent 10 minutes
untangling
allows intangible joy
in the jails of a quiet world

and while we
whirl about campus
when our work- study isn't working
despite procrastination administrations
and discretions against our generation
just know
there's a song for all of that
so get your soundtrack right
cuz i got my music
I got the music
I got the music

just
like
music.

February,
again.

We
scratched the ornaments
glittered deep in the evening
shattered
at the evergreen bottom
slept through the Eve
awakened to unbox a day
seamlessly decorated
Into holly jolly happenstance

Dolled and dressed our tree
skirt every mistake
defaulted to the
new
dreams of the coming year

the holidays are done

Where is my pastor when
I need
more
christmas magic?

where
Is
family
when December
runs out of joy?

Its February
I'm still broke
your promise
        is still broken.

awakened in wonder
nested silently
while whirls of raging fell about me
encompassing stress and aches and downings
flung to the floor
near desert drownings
but amidst the sands came sounds delighted
bubbled and grained eighth notes
passion
subsided the seas of which serpents were fighting
beneath the treasures of the dusty and timid
the melody swayed me
seasoned to rest
and engulfed the dry seas
withholding the breath
above the refrains and chambers of keys
plunging the powerful prostrated sense
granular pieces, ragtime harmonies
mounted the mania
tearing the peace
pouring poisons and toxins
hydrating the quintessence, defrosting me
allowing the movement
tempting the breeze to schlep inspirations
of dancing feet
and the phlange took cadency
bending and swinging
crushing the irritant, shaking aches to defeat
and I grasp what was life, through recreancy
rising from the floor
falling with the beat.

"Read This when you need a pep talk"

You are a beautiful person, no matter how many times you tell yourself otherwise. Your smile, your spirit, your body, and your mind are beautiful. Every shade of you is perfect because you shine so brightly. Celebrate yourself. You have enough. You do enough. Today and everyday you are enough.

I know you're tired. You're carrying hundreds of years on your back, but you still wake up and keep going. You have lots of responsibilities but you still manage, even when it feels like Whack-A-Mole. You have people relying on you- and it's scary to think about sometimes, but you boss up and get shit done. You do work hard. You work very hard, and you do what's needed and then some. Even when you're beaten down you still have heart, and you use your heart for others. We see you. I see you. Thank you for your work. If no one tells you, then I will. Thank you for the work you put into your life that ultimately makes this world turn.

You are where you need to be right now, but you won't stay there for very long. There is more to you. There is always more for you.

I know you're down sometimes, but you've never been out. You've been in crisis before, but you made it through. Sometimes you had to cry. You've had to go at life alone. You've had to break away from what everyone else told you to do. You've had to create something out of nothing to get where you are- but you did it anyway. You persevered, as you always do. You can laugh about it now. You're stronger than anyone else knows or believes. You inspire me with your bravery. You are a hair-flip away from world domination, and the world can't stand it.

It takes strength to get up and go to work every day. It takes power to lift others up even when you don't always have enough to lift yourself. It takes strength to love those around you. Every relationship you have is work, and it takes courage to keep them. It takes tenacity to be vulnerable and be loved. It takes strength to believe in your ability and then go out into the world to prove yourself. You do it every day and that is amazing. That's magical.

There's magic when you speak. There's magic in your word. There's triumph in your ways. There is confidence in your steps because you own every room. There's joy in your presence because you bring you to the table. You no longer show up and stay silent. You bring down the house. It's your time. There's love for you. There's hope for you. There's appreciation for you.
There's nobody on this Earth like you.
Celebrate yourself. Take pride in who you are right now while the rest of us are forced to sit back and watch you slay. Nobody does you like you, and they never will.
Own your magic.

You can't make up
　　　For lost time
But you can love me anyway

You crave
　　　Moments
To be
　　there
I have a hard time
Giving those
to you
Giving those
　　to anyone

I have been hurt before
　　　　I only bet on myself

I know you're proud
I know I disappoint

I don't always reach for you
　　　first

It's new
change is frightening
when change has always meant
instability

there are layers
I want
this moment

Whatever it ends up being

because I love you

Don't ever
        think otherwise
again

"What Happened?"

We don't talk.

our family tensions
        coiled
stretched wide
like kudzu

we thought they were small
        potted problems

with throngs of rain
        sunning
we grew
        Silent and relentless

the blowing mass
of chaos
in chlorophyll
whipping the breeze
edged true North
up
and over tallest tree

here we sit
without harmony

our backs curled South
In the wind

Naked: A Suicide Reply

Sit
naked
talk with me
nervous is unnecessary
for we are clothed with time
dressed in our lifestyles
covered by our aspirations
quilting what we are
at
this moment

Be not weary of wrinkles
they prove your experience
show no concern of crow's feet
our eyes have seen low
Reside refined in one another's presence
no one taints
this moment
    but us

you can cry here
because my heart is held open for you
inhibitions rest about your words
my mind holds you under the stars
so I may gaze at this magnificent human
trapped in garments of humanity

I can love you
naked
I
can see
    you
for the first time
each troubled hair on your arm
the lifelines on your palms
every shade of mahogany that consumes your shape

you are beautiful

you
are
beautiful

with a cold world at your feet
by the achievements that dwell waist-side
beneath the insecurities on your lips
know
my every element adores you
say
I will
see you tomorrow
be
naked with me and find peace

listen,
you are not alone.

Strange Fruit

I've been swinging
breeze tickled my face
long enough to feel
the difference in the air we breathe

weightless
when I check the black box
when I have an opinion to voice
I'm "angry"
when my television keeps
urging
me to be a few shades lighter
when my life had to include a hashtag to get your attention
when I work twice as hard for half the recognition

I'm swinging
whirling through the day

when I can't just be your friend
I have to be your "black" friend with caveats and humor
I'm swinging to appease you
I'm swinging to make you comfortable
I'm swinging just to have the option of an opportunity you never
had to hope for
and this wind is heavy
a tossed body
on a rainy night
wind stings my sunburnt flesh
wilting creases
lightless eyes

I'm swinging in silence
Because we all have a voice but I may not always use it
If it means losing years of playing the game

It's the truth

I hang here
neck slinked in the trees
body dancing in the umbrella limbs
to gasp
A bit of air
        they breathe.

Open Letter to My Own Hair

I did not love you like I should have
for a long time.

See, you were tied to everything else. The pain of bullying. The
memory of not having enough money to get your hair done and
having to ask "favors." Favors I can only repay in company.

You were tied to

cut throat stylists with sharp tongues. Braiders from OtherLands
who mother but never nurse hair.

You were tied
to being told you "weren't going to be a professional."

You were tied
to a box I thought I needed to fit in so that I would always be
neutral.

You were tied
to years of needed forgiveness.

You were tied
to a life I used to know and hate

Meanwhile, you were there. In silent strength anyway.

I am untying you. I am sorry

I love you

I want to love us right.

then we told the world that
everything
was wrong with it
and nothing
was wrong with us

we never asked its opinions
we adapted our faces
to our circumstances
and laced
neck ties with neons
skinnies with band tees
Adderall,
ripped us down hallways
switching friends swapping hobbies
stunted to silence under fluorescent lights...

til we could forget why we were here
when no one gave us answer

when safe was sorry
and scene was seen
and lights meant truth
and we were content in lying
in the black row of an auditorium
shaken, snorting, fixated on the times we hurt
life we suffered
and days survived but never lived
because of this family
or that X
checkered

with fractured faces
shattered Converse
counselor's notes back to class
cryptic with hypercriticism
With bangs too bright and a past too dark
clothes too thin to cover our "tattoos"
wrist too feeble to write words more than poetry
nails blackened to show our drudgery
our image cried help
with no one to save us
as our hearts bled screamo
til our ears rang anonymity

we created this place

I'm an expert with boxes
flip fold forget
I'm an expert
I can mold them
compartmentalize my life into
just a few
I have a talent
I can shift and move my days like Tetris
I can stack my fears of
not having a home
into the boxes
I can fold my wonder
I can mix the separates
I can mislabel anxiety
as long as there are boxes

I can squeeze between the day at school in boxes
I can get bullied off the bus and throw my homework in boxes
I can throw bags into boxes too
as long as my toys aren't lying on the street like before
I can tuck security in boxes
I can claim a church for boxes
I can roam the street with bags
Because boxes have a different place
Boxes have U-Hauls
Boxes have rich friends with trucks
Boxes have storage units
Boxes have closed garages with shiny bikes.

I just want boxes
with stickers, and tape and big markers.
forgetting a past is a box of its own
We had bags.
luggage with broken zippers
all too familiar with being scraped down the street
Bags.
we pushed all the uncertainty
deep in the bottoms
Gym bags, grocery bags, drawstring bags,

Trash
Bags.

My Barbie feet would poke through to the cold air through the
bag every time
at least on those nights we had something in common

shapeless lifeless bag
hopeless bag
I grab the end tabs
lift and kick it through the door
type bag
because at 7 and a half the burden is heavy
at 9 and a half the burden is heavy
at 10, and 12, and 13,and 15 the burden is heavy

at 26 the burden is heavy
I count the days down til the move
I called the movers 26 times
To make sure they're coming
with boxes
I walk my hallway waiting for a knock so I don't have to touch
all my bags that are still there
My bags piled to the ceiling fan
overflowing out the door
my bags hoarding a mind unseen
my bags with red drawstrings and bills poking through
my bags with lost memories and quiet neighbors
my bags with family, with guilt of success, peace-less
my bags filled with constant fear of becoming unstable

you can't move your mindset because there are bags in the way
the meal comes but the roof doesn't there's bags in the way
the calls come and you give your last $20 there's bags in
the way

Gym bags, grocery bags, drawstring bags, trash bags.

they sit me down
make me
    unpack
they sit
under my eyes until
    I put them
Down
wherever I belong

Acquainted

We may never meet
our
eyes swell the same
our mouths hollow
for same airs
our backs sweat
in quietude of hunger

words grow tired
on unread pages

We need you.

I'd rather them root
into your rich soils
press your shoulders
deep in the evening
warm in commonality

I'll harvest memories
My words
My hearts poeting
        as mined gold
or rather
as smoothed pebbles
glistering
the creeks
of your reverence

So let me
  Come in

           Please, remember Me.

all I want
Is
to Make space
in this moment
with you

"Please Don't Ask me About Work"

I asked my client
        Why she drank
Pine-Sol

She said

"I couldn't
afford an abortion"

                Social Work is heavy work

Everyone else's trauma
 Sits
Right
        On top
Of my own

That's where the Passion is.

I asked my client

What she wanted for Christmas

She said
"a parent,
        any parent will do"

I asked my client
tell
the happiest day of their life

They said

"when you came to
    my house
and put me in foster care"

            Social Work is heavy work.

I do not always have the right answers but I try
to have the safest answer that's honest

I will not lie to your children for you
they deserve the best you can give
even if it's a call saying you aren't coming

we've been sitting in this parking lot for hours
waiting

I cannot show up for them like you
the department will never be a parent

children
covered in scabies
Reach for me

Reach for anyone

children
break
In courtrooms

children
ache in
a parent's broken promise

parents
believe boyfriends
over daughters

Or lose touch in jail from a visitation window

I've seen the world raw
Before it comes on the local news
3 days later

parents
slump
in euphoria
lost to narcotics

I am tired of trying to sit you up.

parents
watch their child
die
at the hands of lovers

May they all rest in peace

I've seen it all, but I need rest too

      Social work is heavy work

We can't talk about
     My day
Over dinner

You are not ready
     to hear
how dark
the world can be

scuffed boots
hung
tightly to the tapping feet
shifting dirt on the dusty breezeway

a lazy melody
drifted through
the 89-degree Carolina evening

his Levis were worn
thin as linen
torn about his scabbed knee
below his flannel shirt
with "many holes for many days"
and just the same
his bandana was the hue of survived elements

of
all of the things
that appeared to be out of touch
to those who passed by
according to his whistle
that stretched
past the parking lot
and across a coral sky
all was well

"I'm doing quite alright," he said

"I really can't complain."

They touched

Me
    wrong

too soon.

 instead of becoming angry

I became a Social Worker

Yes, I forgive you.

That is

    Grace.

Diabetes

our friendships are
    Convenient
overpriced
    available
to all
who wander this aisle

we have items for you.
Love in chocolate. Lust in Warheads.

Be sour about us.

our cashiers are closing shop.
they turn the lights off

Oh, I forgot something.

we always forget something
we didn't own what's missing.
food won't solve this

but candy
will make my heart beat a bit faster
to catch up with my misfortune

She's run slow for long
She's hefty train and rice
She's exploratory, reluctant to be herself

knock her upright
let's buy candy
be kids like we want to be
without rules and bills

sorrow made to sugar

I need
a convenient friendship

I Grow Weary

I fell today
and maybe it was
my steps
my footing
my unlikeliness to look down
though it seems I have been
staring at the path for quite some time
was it my shoes
their journeyed soles
freshly found laces
that have been pressed to the backsides
of the flimsy tongues
Was it?
I cascaded in the winds of my imagination
to acquaintance the final Canto of my mind
am I not to walk
in my self-made maze
of emotional greenery
and fragile mosses of time
am I not to walk?
in sickness
in strides of regret
or regression
each paced pain
mustering the dusts of my contemplation

I grow weary.

I grow timid
flourishing in browning leaves
of brittle shinings
unlike my likings
laying here
under brush and berry
to find shade
on the treaded walkways of my introspects.
Must these plants die
alongside my logic
to diminish the flowering
of what was thought to be genuine
but only serves as a sacrificed spectacle
of that that lives in me?

I grow weary.

weeding life
through ill-found vineyards
nestled past the ways
of those who never noticed
the dying perennials
or climbing ivy that uphold the house beneath it

I grow weary.

must it rain
for me to live
for ivy to grow
for honeysuckles to fill
under the delicacy of its petals
must I fall
to be swept in the currents
of my own irrigations
to help those who must always have my pruning?

I grow weary.

A$AP Rocky & My walk to the store for Peach Nehi

under the pretty
never forget

that I am hood AF
just like them

understand we come from the same place
just because I wear nigga shit better
doesn't mean I am more or less deserving

This is where we talk about it.

I am not "a little bit" Black for you.
That's not how this works.

I
        understand
I can be intimidating

but you fear me
your knee jerk terrors
are fatal   for us

know your injustices

undermine the idea
the medium skinned non-threatening Black woman that I am

comes with history.
comes with a case
comes with a rougher edge than you expect

I am a Capital fuckin' G.
I gel my edges just the same.

I was taught not to wear my circumstances on my sleeve.
And I
        dress
          Well.

The Impossible Woman (Slam)

I am a woman
It's almost impossible

The gold in our blood
Makes our feet
      Fall
Heavy
    Sometimes

the curve in our spine
swells from carrying my burdens and yours too
I am a woman
It's almost impossible
my neck cranes in angst
for a single day of mutual respect
 I am woman
     In sound
In color
     In shape
In this reality
I am
woman striving
restless in achievement
dazzling you from the back row
waking
the lessons of lifetimes

I rub my palms
touch your chest
there is strength there
a beating drum of shamanic order
a vibration transcendent of all things
the fibers of all importance
the immaculate conception unrealized
the undertaker of Overbearers
the Odyssey of endless stories
the sleeping lion with a beautiful mane

You.

You touch me
You wear heels like you fucking mean it
You melt this world
widdle paint off of the walls when you walk
Baby
You
     Take
Space.

You
Take
     His
Space

remind us of your sacred church
You ooze divinity from your pores
imprison insecurities in aged pews
You
    Glisten
You change tides
You are sea
You are skies
You take shape
reaching up and out and around and beneath us
shaking earths below the sea
Sweetie
You are matchless magic

A time traveling
Energy shifting

Goddess of the Day
In
    All
Ways
I am a woman
And with all this
    badassery

It's
Almost impossible

    Almost.

My Last Drink for a Very Long Time

only sorry
    When I drink
     Hennessy
when the
coaster sticks
to the bottom

I tilt
spiced sorrel dreams
in my glass

pretend I
diwn't
miss you.

I hope I make you proud.
I hope you love me just as much as you did when I was 6
and
you were invincible.

She is flawless.

In the books of denial
she reads me beautiful lies
pestilence fancies my ears

she holds me under her words
twists me beneath the consonants
slurring syllables in my spine

we speak no language
        but deception
graze eyes over the pages
of spoken scripts

I tousled these dreams
of shifting dread
upholding the paperback forgery
aside the "x" of the false

and beneath a signature
of the betrayed
            lies
the preface
of fallacy.

What It Means to Be "A Man" (Slam)

Underwear are stupid
they have no real purpose
but to annoy
deploy wreck twist
make us
conditioned
to the idea that we can always be slightly inconvenienced
For the sake of some man's ego

A contraption
To highlight what is already alluring
And soft
      And everything

See
Vagina runs the world
we may not want to say it out loud

But she does
And so I will
And so mine will
And she speaks

Truth

She knows nights of stroking egos

underwear
and taking them off
is the sweet
     of that moment

there's is power in here
the gravid dense perfect
Ph balanced
nectarous vagina

maybe you don't know your own
because you are sparing someone's feelings

Dump him
Dump him

we deserve good sex just like everyone else.
We masturbate
    a lot. I know.
We don't talk about it
we know
smell one another all the same

Sex energy is the most powerful energy the human body can
manifest for itself next to Enlightenment.

Sit on that.

Spread that
Lick that
Groom that
Cherish that

someone entering my body means
I have allowed you into

the most revered
          organ on Earth

your vagina stops time
your vagina makes them make poor decisions
your vagina has a mind of her own

your vagina
is bigger

There.
There you go.

Your vagina is bigger.

Does that make sense?

women don't sit around
and swap big dick stories
We don't have time
to make every conservation
A battle of egos

For them its up or not
For us

There's levels to this shit

There's "pre and post period" vagina
There's "did I drink enough water to long-haul this sex?" vagina
There's "this isn't good, way less motion in the ocean" vagina
There's "fuck, already?" vagina

The Unsatisfied.
             She is
Salty.

That is truth.

what do you

think you

taste like, sir? Sweet Tea? No, Exactly.

        Exactly.

we change our diets to taste good to you.

And what do you do?
Hope?

Exactly.

Everything isn't about you.
Everything isn't about your dick.
Everything doesn't end when you're done.

That's the most trash shit I have ever

Done.

That's it
That the end of the poem because I got all I needed
I wasted your time and walked

But I want to be macho
So I will walk around your apartment naked
I'm big tough guy
For what?
For fucking what?

As a woman I have tried to understand what it means to be

"A Man"

　　　　　and at its core
Being "A Man" is nothing

Vaginas are bigger than manhood
Whatever the fuck that means
So just
　　　ENOUGH
Let go of this idea
That you are supposed to do XYZ
your friends aren't here

To watch this.

They are not here to fuck me
And they won't be here to love me.
They are not here to love you back.

They are not here to bless you with our vagina

I'm not here to embarrass anyone
But if it stings
Its sticks.

But I'm not sorry.

Get it together.

Let down this wall and just be here.
All the way here

Down here
And there
And all the way down
To the underwear
I didn't wear.

Yes.
That.
Exactly.

Vagina stops time.

Why Self-publish?

Yes, it's art.

But it's also my only child.
It's my Baby.

It needn't
be
touched.

Someone will read this and publish later works for me.

I manifest that.
But not for this one.

This is my heart.
My life on page.
I don't want your edits. Keep them.

You cannot edit Me
You cannot edit Freedom
You cannot edit Life.

I have been nesting.

It's my Moment.

No one gets to touch it,

I'm sorry.

I am done nesting.

I'm not sorry

I won't apologize for doing
Exactly
What I want
Or saying
What I want
Or living
How I want
Or making a grand gesture

As I make New Life.

Yes, it's Art.
But it's also my baby.

My truest labor of Love.

I mothered

Acquainted

The first
Golden Child
of many.

The Lovers

The Purple Wonderful

Yes

I Am A Goddess.

but
no.
I'm allergic to the grapes

......you'll want to feed me.

I am Earth

Peace.
        Home under your skin.

I speak through you

I touch you
        across the ether.

You do my work for me.

You bend in the thought.

I waste days

wondering
how long you're gonna pretend I'm not there.

It's an honest rub

curled toe in a narrow dream

I am lightning

punishment
wrapped bliss

You won't forget me
I
melted
you

Into tomorrow

these spaces are vast as heaven

let's talk sweetness

I'm bigger than any thought you could have.

bigger than time.
yes. I fucking know.

a dirty future

I'm big as fuck.

perfect harmony in a place unknown.

but once you know

I stick

I shape you
        blind

My love is

Magic

True Magic

the sort that snakes down your back
in the waiting
        on the tocking

Miss me, bitch.

I am butter.
I am Dreams.

you can't
stop having me
as easily as you thought.

Us is a perfect
Balance

Remember I was perfect.
Remember I was perfect.
Remember I am perfect.

Because I Am.

Us is
        Balance
and
        you still
taste
        Me.

No Title

You can't see my ocean
As you stand in my water

             You can't love me.

You took my art
my creative
my ended spirit

And I ached

Days went

       Left

Tomorrow feels like
An eternity away
From hope

I
cringed
in this
house

I
shrank
in this
house

You have never
been
        Loved before
You have
never
felt
        Whole.

Your
Love
and love lost
was
conditional

and you
Ached
in this house.

I tried to nurture it into you
Give
My all

        my Soul.

but

        I don't want flowers.

I want you to get help.

the worst
        things
about us
brought
us

Here.

are these my mountains?
Does she hurt like this?
How can she move
In space so free
can we tame
monsters in convulsion

    I cave me

Up
  How can we dream?
Do I arch my back like you would think?
a blessing
I'd break my spine for you

Love
Me

as monster in dreams
We're home inside each other

Sweetest. Let's dream Pumpkin

Dream
    Up

roll your eyes through me I miss you
Fuck

yes
For us
Everything

every. thing.

drip

    us
this

Every
    Thing.

In the Mind

    feel
pain
    in this life

but

decide
whether you choose

to
    suffer.

When you answer my questions with questions

I tried to
stretch my imagination
to a time
    when you cared

I was delusional

You don't have
     the neuroplasticity.

Satin's Situation

dress me according
lying's my design
flourishing, faulty, fabricated
decorated in decadent deceptions
pestilent patterns penetrate erratic ears
only eye sensing seams
caught
between cuff and calamity
a seamstress' premise above accentuated alterations
avoiding altercations
regurgitated ruffles
measure my demise
unraveling yesterday
seeming seaming to satin situations
tainting tapestry
upon a mannequin's mastery
"to them I can lie"

Beg

Love me

my heart
can whisper no louder
than my touch

Love me

my eyes die
to live in your thought

Love me

my hands throw
repentance
beneath forgotten novels

Love me

I waft
the religion of your existence

Alternative Lifestyles

Freedom is cloak
   Austere, class

Don't fucking. Touch.
 Me.

     Yet.

Your hands have too many questions.

Your souls are pink
Mauve.
ripening in curiosity

     Come closer

I list my needs in your eyes.

give

And you will Give to me.

It's a
wrangling
dream.
We
swell over seconds.

You write.
I write.

Putrid in honesty
Fresh and adult

"I loved last night, yeah. So whe-"

"Yes, I'll see you soon."

As Tainted Oxygen

Respiration is my handicap
    vitality
vice

Air left my lungs in your sight
    as my eyes
swallowed
       each concept of your matchlessness

Why must I need to breathe?

vaporize
beneath the exhalation
of your name on my lips
dissipate to the ceiling
idle, evanescent

all six senses
     fail
    me

suffocating my logic
to elevate
    hallucination
of contentment

asphyxiate
me.

"What is your sexual orientation?"

If a true bisexual
you will always have
          that problem

Partners believe
they can never
be
all you want

because they can't be your everything

That is true
They cannot.

I am the only one that can do that.
You are the only one that can do that.

No one can be my everything

I don't think about her while I am with him
I don't think about him while I am with her

It's connection
with person
as the person
          they are

                    no sex or gender considered

I like

Them as they are

honor boxes they chose to check

I love the skin and bones of   You

There is no side
          to pick.

DJ Cosmic Sex

your "jumblings" are genius
fine
melty and iridescent

requiem
requests
of days lost
to
silence

your pieces
are tinkered tracks
fixtures
of New Sound spaces
That's your Places.

Make more noise.

catalog calamity
lines written are bountiful creations
filling books on the mantelpiece
of my contemplation
actions are
      nameless comics
gesticulations
     of yesterday's News

today, you are a narrative
two eyes and one soul
spark the synonyms of subtitled synopsis
tripled my temptation
grasping guilt amidst the shelves

Can I find you here?

Among the readied rows of reading
stuck
      stale
        stagnant

magnanimous collections of you
yearning pages of Paradise Lost
periodicals paralyze
building
library of selective memory
parables stand as perceptual entity
decimalized
contentment rummaged
answers shoved by archives

You are a volume loved
lengthy, lofty
cajoling content
lifting novelties novel
perplexed in realms of unsolved texts

I
    find
You
bending back covers
of my copyrights

Hold Your Applause

Its not 'just an orgasm'

Its every blood cell echoing under your skin

and the Power of Control

reaches through him
reaches through her
reaches through them

and the pang of weakness in ecstasy

pours the bed

fills
    the
      room.

the neighbors are clapping.

Pheromones

I
 smell
    Her

on You.

There is

        Nothing
    Else
To say.

Be cold

        on Your side

of Our bed.

To Fluoresce

she illuminates me
across the dawn
    of placid shadows

her truth collapses the sun

the glow
of falling day
lapse sensation about the heart
pleasure about the dimming
peace beneath the glare
of lambency

she came
   with
    me
into the hollows of fulfillment
picturing endearment
in the face
    of empty frames
losing me
    in the battle of imagination
to chase
illustrious dreams
tasted contemplations
   indulged
in the dimming glint of
her embrace

Open Letter to My Next Partner

I did not always have it all
I know what its like to go without
I work hard
I am extremely hard on myself

for awhile
I was the only one
being hard
    Or being anything
On Me.

I dislike my voice
yes, I can sing
If you never force me to sing
I will sing all the time.

Angles
I am chameleon
I blend
    stand out when necessary.

I love Goldfish
    I eat copious amounts of Goldfish
It's nostalgic, and I want to be a child at heart forever

This is me.
    Be Kind

I am just like you
our paths will cross
at the most inconveniently convenient time
lean into faith and fate.

If you have read this far
You are halfway in my door already.

Invitation by John Coltrane 1959

It's better for my ears
how
the Music traveled
    me
disrobed
honest moments
were my ears not good enough for you?
I listened
I was scared
    now I know
when the answer needed to be no
some No's
     have layers

find me
you found me
honesty

The mistake of the moment
helped you find me
let you know

Can we go have sex now?

I'm this honest
my nipples perk
hurt
confirm what you wanted to know
honestly

Can her body be truth as mine?
Can she know what it's like to go beyond
The pleasures
I
    feel
for you and you And you

I know my body's honesty
drippy
    sweaty
marvelous

Show me the honesty of you
Have you cared for him?
He's bone heavy tired

and I love him
and we can love her

Rub my ass
In the morning baby
Wake up
Roll close in the morning baby

truth, let's be honest.

syrup and majesty
skip luck in atrophy
life supped
your eyes don't know where to start

honestly.

My ego is big as yours
my Priscilla is sweet as yours
promise me
you will fold me in half
drape me over your shoulder

Smack that.

ankles dangle
humbly

I can't go anywhere like
this
you like
        that

Honor me.

My chest deflated in touch

destroy the
me

that you have seen on the internet
I need to feel
        the powers that be

Are mine
Through
        Mastery

I grew tired of dimming
For company

We are watching me

Honest

I won't flinch
an audience is

home on me

hot warm
relief
ecstasy

swirl night sweet
next in me

I'm honestly

extending three invitations

You know who you all are.

Come with me?

I take you higher
These thighs shake honey
    Honest
Honestly

She is free
And
     Rude
But not sorry

I heard me
Fuck, she's nasty
The classy sexy
Is just
     another
mask of me

Honestly

You caught a cramp
In your legs

"adulting" sex

    Tire of me
Make your rounds
I think I need more of you.
Oh, and You.

Honesty

put me here in your story
stir that story
Read
    with me?

case your eyes my letters
I spelled everything
and the tip

Honestly
    wet dream speeches
And
     Hominy
Clobbering knees
Naked

Licked
complete

enjoyably.

I goofy smile when I'm done
I made   messes
        Watch your eyes
I have manners
I say thank you

Humbly.

My honest is good in your ears
Your body sang in me
not casual but we tried

Comfortably

We slow slid and fit
Comfortably

Slid and fit
Comfortably

Slid
Slid
Slid
I fit you, each

     somewhere

Comfortably.

A Hand in a Half Empty Pocket

raced through traffic
left
    my
friends
      early

for You

I open

on rainy Tuesday

with left sweet
markings

we are each other's problem and solution.

deeper than us

deepest to you

Marry the Night

I married
        The Night.

Took my life

Down damp back alley
My ties
        Stretched
until I was poet, loosed

I unleashed her here.

The truth I've come to cradle
press through my chest
into yours

I felt you and your everything.
        your forevers.
humidity and desire

I am
the water of you with days to live in here.

You haven't felt immensity

tour me
        your
cities.

I married the night

For
You

someone
speaks life
deeper than my bones
bellows
love into my digits
I ingest
every sip
of an untucked bottom lip
lift
the ceiling
to the highs of my infatuation
relax you
somewhere
wearing the time
left rough in the rubble
to smooth all of your edges

let's
     just
chill

loop Lupe
fasten the ribbons of midnight

and

be gifts
to one another
in
morning

she
    must
be
my favorite getaway
our past two moments
    lost
have found me
and we have yet to find
    home

Are We Soul Mates?

He never said

"I think you're
beautiful"

He didn't ask
me
on a date

He said
with no tone

"I like your handwriting"

and
that
was

All.

Tay-Row

We have been around

Each other
So long

We have our
own language

Inside jokes
for
Inside jokes

You get me

sometimes
too
well
And I get
Angry

even though you are right

We speak in Oneness
I miss our Sound

Today you are beautiful

Flawed
        Opened

raw.

I get to see you
        Seeing Yourself

the most beautiful thing
I have
ever

known.

Prompt: Write a short rhyme with big words.

The muffled plangent
of my hearts murmured tangent
beat slow
stagnant
to the warmth of the breeze
and I
thwarted, lofty
regarded you
softly
the outre of your presence
put wind in the trees

Until Its You (Slam)

It's so gradual
It's not outright

It's bending
for love
      until you forget
              how to stand up straight
What do
    I
want to eat?

What do
    I
want to wear?

You don't notice it
 at first

It's so gradual.

You find a hobby
 they hate it

I stop.

Respect and Love, right?

I always have an opinion
But I hold it in
          Just for today
It's not worth the argument.

It's so gradual

You don't realize how you
          were
silenced

You just know it's better
          when you are

It's so gradual

Time goes by
          We go with it

What are
          My
goals?

What do
I
want to do
     next?

It's quieter
If they
          think for me

I don't want to fight

They are not doing it on purpose but
          It hurts
All the Same.

Before you know it you're alone

          in a new way.

Everyone can see you suffering but no one wants to disrupt
what looks good otherwise

It all looks good.

Perfect is Safe.

I was perfect
          As whoever they wanted

But I was no one

I was not me.

You find yourself

At the

   Bottom
   Of
   A
   Well

Looking
    Up
Hoping someone
Will stop by and truly listen

But seasons pass
Rains come
Holidays pass
Moves come

I reach up.

But it's never high enough for you to see my weary hand
Until I am told I

Don't
    Have
Hands

And eventually you start to believe it.

It's so gradual.

What is my worth?
Do I have value?

Sometimes it's a little
Sometimes they say none

    "Worthless"
It's so gradual
You are a house
Being eaten
By termites
Crumbling from the inside out
It's so gradual

      They played me my own 911 tape.
      I can never un-know my own Suffering
It's so gradual

Until it
Goes
Too
Far.

Now we're somewhere else
My brain is somewhere else
I escaped inward instead of
Reaching
    Out.
The poster says "if you need help reach out"

I have
reached
    out
Until my arms fell from my body
Until my face left my face
Until my stomach folded in exhaustion

I reached

Until my knees shattered carpet

Until my
    Chest
    Fell
To dust

Until there was nothing left to fall
Until I was nothing
We Are Not.

And Everyone
  was somewhere else

It's so gradual

when you Go.

But when you decide to leave
You are still silent

You have not heard your own thought in years
Your own voice is foreign
You're heavy in your step
You still want to be told what to do sometimes
But you know its wrong

But that's been your life for so long

It's so gradual

you never thought it
Could
 be you
until it Was you.

It's so gradual

You build courage

You pull newness out of your frame

You rebuild

You climb from the bottom

You fill
    your own well.

You make your home a home.
You find home safe in your skin

It's so gradual

Your truth overflows you
Someone believes you
And the bricks that sat heavy on your back

Made you strong enough to build a fortress

It's so gradual

You build that house
And grief
Can't afford to stay long

It's so gradual

You stand up slowly
But you
    Stand

It's so gradual

Your Roar.
You sing life back into your bones
You fill the room
With an Essence

And you never let anyone

Take it away.

It's so gradual

To say

I went through
This shit

But
Today I stand up straight.

Placebo: A Dating Experiment

pill raced through me
tumbling torrents down my esophagus
seasoning acids thrashing
coaxing my cranial complexes
vexing my expectations
cajoled to this fallacy
a beneficial belief
that this samples substitute convolutes my being
circumstances entranced me.

Drugged am I.

He covered confounds
amplified my statistical significance
in the noise of experiment
every element
balanced beside enthralling equations
reversed revised requirements
mentally matching attacking designs
aside my mind.

Drugged, am I?

Doubtfully, I digress
distress the matter-of-factorial tutorial
I have no knowledge of
my passions flashing skewed data about the observations

debrief me.

Her voice
    liquid sound
shifting memories
forward in curves of time

she dreams me like a summer
    peach comfort
    opens my day
in her night

a weathered curtain
still in endless mornings

I miss peace
when
I wake up in the clouds

Obsessed

I want to drink your water.
That's love.
a worship in the unknown
We don't speak this love out loud
She's left and caramel
pulls are loud
an animal need
steadily etching over primal
to hungry space
In morning sweat off lazy sex
that is the loud
In the pulling
A worship unknown
We tucked
    souls in an abhorred place
smell your weaknesses
I ache
to relieve
    muster clear
from
fall and rise of You

yes
    be
Home

on
 me

I Used to Love Someone

I looked outside.
I looked at my calendar
realized that I hadn't changed the month
I just wanted it to be November
forever.

I miss us.

if I could fit my ego between
blue lined paper
it would resemble
distorted persuasive essay
thesis
and our conclusion.
if someone told me that
my efforts could reach you
and
enrich your eyes with its findings
I
could be us.

Us.
not a complicated situation
not a hook-up
notable structure
that held substance
November remembrance

Us.

I miss us.
I don't miss the pain.
I don't miss the dysphoria.
I don't miss the illusion I placed here for your errors.
I just miss us.
because "us" was safe
and proud
and mistakenly first.

Us was love.
loved was I
if measured in miles
it would span every sunless sea.

You loved me
despite the pressure set beneath our history
despite 'her'
you loved me.
If I could twist my mind to believe otherwise
the malice of the disorder would paralyze me

Everyday
I ache
for paralysis.

To My Diaphanous Lover:

Please don't touch me. Our centers have divided and the nucleus of this atomic nuisance trifles me. Stifles me to a dysphoric disaster known as love.

Please avoid this cranial contortions fortunes, the gimmick of the limitless wealth of what cannot be. My pathos configured paralysis of parse thought, thwarting my expectations past paroxysm.

I have no sayings as to what may bound from my limbs, what may spill from my mouth, what may pull at the diffidence that diffuses what stands as my heart.

Please, take closure in this closing I am unfitting fiction to this fairy-tale fallacy we've fit into this satisfying sense of synapse collapsing my Nervous wisdom.

Systems have failed me.

Being Little

I know
that
     feeling

when Someone
you trust
really hurts you
and that hurt
swallows you up

and makes you
     small.

I know that feeling
Deep
and   close

I love words
but there are

no words
    for
   that
moment

now you know
how much
      I
know
    about
Heartbreak.

I Call Her "Priscilla"

Yesterday
    I was lavender and velvet
I slinked on the Sexy
coated your throat
since
your face was
    the best seat in the house.

    Hahahah.

I drip sex.

somedays it's radiate
    horned
      auroral
casting flashes and shadows
Shudder in purple sheets

somedays it's Power
pulse in your temple
I am naked again

I am wearing you
 You
      fit
        tight
some days it's effervescent
lofty, spacious
I lift air for you here
Breathe your bigness
into me

lets be body art
A Saturday morning muse

See us.

somedays I am altruist
I
    want
you
     Gifted

Unravel all I carry
I am not too heavy

her name is Priscilla
she tugs ecstasy
through the Members
of the private church of my bed.

somedays I dribble
    glide
You levitate
lets
      never
come back

My body holds your Everything
we
    travel
you go
     blind

I come
    everywhere

let's get it

everywhere.

I'm Still Salty. Fuck you.

Memories are thick.

I hope they twinge
   in the marrow
of your speckled bones
    rattle
every dexterous movement
of your being
until
    you

Forget
every other girl

I am
here
we have been here

red and unhinged

deeper
than what's comfortable.

Mahogany

turn
    your
Back
on me
    chocolate exudes your spine
travel, touch, taste
    terrain of each vertebrae
to journey
    the mount
against my fingers
elevates senses to senselessness
    ease me
on peaks of euphoria

move
mountains.

Prison Broke

its been two days...

despite the spectrums
that separate our colors
fathomed in the afflictions
of prism premise
I am pressed
atop the mirrors

to speak of you.

the utterance
escapes my esophagus
lust
straddled my misery of your absence
sentencing me to the prisons of my mind
wind
up somewhere near
the flow
going against gravity
an entity when you touch me
leaves me
light-footed

pounding hearts
silent screams
escape the eyes
      of those who cry out
the last tear
      of pain

from shards of a fractured heart

glare
beyond shadows case
past gleams of reason
and find light
in the starless oasis

"She's A Victim"

It's like
    waking up
from 17 dreams at once

of a mind game
you didn't know you started playing

one you
    didn't ever choose
but you have

somehow

altered your existence
    to play

It's my go.

Aviator

Despite our perfect pleats
there is no we
and
If I were skilled in origami
I would fold yesterday into tomorrow,
fall in the crease
and take flight in the wings
of a Paper Crane...

since
I fly solo.

I ask God "who?" And He replies "why?"

I've never wanted to believe in anything more than myself,
but, I, too, can fall. And in this case, plummet. But the bottom
is nowhere close, somehow. Impulse has driven me farther
than intellect. Emotions surpass knowledge. And how funny it
is that neither one of these things can be taken, reimbursed,
or hindered. Yet we attempt to detach, regroup, and dissipate
them. Though our surfaces can be spotless no one scrapes
beneath the tiles nor chooses to cleanse our foundation.
Ironically, this exercise cannot be done alone.

The soul
is
malleable...

when in flight.

and so I give you
68 paper cranes
for each day
of our aviation.

My Only Poem About Love of Social Media

This is the part where I get to be petty
I get to
scroll past your photo
and not like it

this is your ignored meme
your sub-tweet
your re-post and unacknowledged tag

I don't want
Whatever it is

I'm an actual person
Not a robot machine for advertising

Unsubscribe me
I don't have time for another
Email funnel sis

They don't want me
    Like
That

They want the raw and unadulterated

                            Well here I am.

I don't care about social media but I got really good at it
and you should pay me for how much I know

But it's pointless

If you don't love yourself
Why should anyone else?

Heal, baby girl.

      Stop scrolling.
you've filtered your esteem away
for a 'like'
an intangible dopamine kick
and when its over
You need another
We can't hold conversation in real life
How disappointing

I like internet you better.
                        You disappear in person
I hate that

So come be you
when you talk to me

Social Media will never make you Whole.

When You Left Me on Read

I'm sorry I keep bugging you.

I lose my mind sometimes in Lonely.

and

I am not proud about it.
I did not want to sit and cry about it alone along with everything
else there is to sit and cry about again.

I'm not trying to guilt you.
I just felt like a loser, lately.
I needed to talk.

I needed to talk.

I'm fucking overwhelmed and scared.
I'm tired of being scared.

Everything feels so much bigger than me and this
new life I have to create
feels far

impossible on days like
today.

I hate myself for feeling little again.

I've lost my mind sometimes in Lonely.
Lonely disease
will make you
 Sick
with
desperation

make others
apologize to
you
for having
    their own life

the curdle in the back of your throat
at an unread text

we do not Lonely
the same

some let lonely
creep through their fingers
    onto Facebook

others lay worlds
In their best friend's ear
On the phone…..again

But me?

I sit in my Lonely
sleep in my worry
of the most harmful human condition
dawn strength like I am not hurting

silent dangerous Lonely
people easily forget
as busy

we go quiet

until me and Lonely leave together

Alone.

So

Please call me
Text me and think about it

I have lost my mind this time in Lonely
And she won't let me leave by myself.

Someone with a Name

To someone,

peel love
off the broken dermis
of objectivity

we cannot stand
as wounds.

To Someone with a name,

we can be lost
    homeless
and relay the message.

when lofts
lose bricks
in the hands of Layers
it is we
who live without homes

desperately
I need shelter

to make amends
in the midst of cracks
growth
in the day of evenings
fear
pulls the foundations
folds roofs
in the groves of the unsettled

build me windows
I may look
        beyond
the faithless

construct my medium
so I may see communications

Mold me home
for I am no longer
a temple
stain the glasses
to tint transparent tapestries
that dance beside tilted frames
wearied on walls

let me fall
again
in the depressions
of forgotten streets.

To Someone,

"give light to my eyes, or I will sleep in my depth"

relieve me in your night
and
knight me in your relief
in the Wars
of us.

True Love

I broke myself
trying to fix her

I crashed

I stumbled out of the wreckage
unconscious
of the day
and the next day
and the next day
and the next day
and the next day

Until I forgot
what the wreck
was for.

How many times will I drive my life into someone else's hurt?

we are a gathering of strangers
the piling collision
of a
broken people

    stumbling

inundated by the sound of metal bending souls.

Fresh From The Fight

I cried hero
and
Love was my savior

I cried hero
to sing you beneath the notes of unfound scales
grace the ears
of the blinded many
those too scared to fear
too lost to feel

I cried hero for you,

bless the heart that bends
the treble of key change
range
blusters above the floor

fearless- as if my mess is just temporary; but you are stationary
I could love you
nothing secondary to that

So I act as if I worry
pray as if I sleep
because I love as if I'll die
unsaved…

I cried 'hero'

And I love.

How Creatives Justify The Crazy

let the Art
    save you
swallow you
sleep you deep on the belly
rest warm in completion

channel
your
trauma
    into a passion project

until it explodes in the reckoning of You.

Art is a weary craftsmanship
Years to oil
    Affix
   detach from
   your hurt
long enough to write it out

the craze is in the show
the wanting for them to find
the lapse of art over artist

So

Let the art take you.

You will always be There.

The Rest

A Poem About Loretta

She texted,

"LOL girl, I'm trying
       to get
   on
your
    Level."

I said,

    "Don't.

      It's Madness up here."

??????????????????????????

let me ease you
into the notion
that I might be from Somewhere Else.

a quiet unfolding
first out of body
then

out of touch

     at will.

Let me ease you
into the notion
I
know more than
I
   will
     ever
   say

I heard your thoughts
slanted intentions
Higher Self
coaxing Fourth Dimension

I know.

I
    Know.

Hold on.

let
      me
ease
    You
in

The Rest is the Madness of Me.

"What is your Nature?"

They are all letters
to myself
from my Places

I don't Stay Here all the time

they are
letters
cursive letters lapping
permissions to be free

beyond the freedom in the moment
as it's happening

I go
    backwards
Steering, sizing myself from
a future standing in a puddle of mud
when pennies made sense
and there was no buzz of electricity to be heard
and everything is made of
what it
says it's made of.

I lean forward
spreading seconds in the Matrix
I warn of overtakings
broken dreamways
Mapping timespace
where the stars are
as untamed pets of the Sky
there's no force in New Utopia
Their Peace and our "peace" are
Different.

Hush.

We don't need to talk about this.

My poem
        says exactly
what
        I
        "mean"

Meanings are fragile in this dimension
Did you catch the Meaning's flying
over your shoulder?

We were Almost All There.

            almost.

lets sing in to Time
see the shockwaves bounce too Soon
Days Later

We don't need "food" here

Spirit loves us in feeding

In.

The Separate Place.

They told me it was my imagination
mental prowess in freed Time
a glitch in seen possibility
an unusual
misunderstanding

A dreamy kid with her head in the clouds.

Well, fuck.
my Imagination keeps Happening
before anyone else
knows I know the Already

I can't Dream this Big by myself.

They told me it was my imagination
but now
I'm almost thirty
my "friends" stand
close
in the Closer
of
Night

That's my
Nature.

a laugh in the Teetering
That's my mind
squeaking as it fucks its Self

That's
My
Nature

one Mind
in two Places.

The Akashi and Sugar

I've had many lives before this one.

I was Voodoo High Priestess
A siren of Port of New Orleans
Wild with absinthe
Passing blessing in my wake
I
Channeled
 God
in work
and prayer
My gowns rustled ethereal
        traced the streets

moved.

My train
        lavish
disrespectfully long

I
turned the paint around
     In
      every
room.

manifested life into the dead,
gripped countless souls
dragged them through lifetimes unknown.

I was gifted.
I blessed. I casted. I scryed. I read.

I was big.
I grew too big.

They feared me.

My children were persecuted before my eyes.

I've had many lives before this

I was one of the first land-owning
women
    in Haiti
I
    Grew
Big
I grew sugarcane
amassed
    loyal slaves
treated them fair for the times

distributing my bounty
           around
                the Worlds
connecting
        last hint in shipment
to Port of New Orleans

I was Domino Sugar before Domino Sugar

I was divinity
but
I got
      lost
I went so deeply into
The Other Side
I never came back
        the
         Same

The house on the hill grew silent.
I lost everything.

And now I have this life

Growing.
Big.
Again.

I want to get it right

        This Time.

The Lioness

Dizzy Dizzy
You must be busy
Trying to figure me out
I'm black and white
Callous, spite
your mouth is fluid spout
Dizzy Dizzy
You must be busy
Calling your friend
To say
That she already knew
What she said I would do
But how did she know
"My" way?
Dizzy Dizzy
You must be busy
Keeping me out of your dreams
The kick and wallow
of Marriage Hollow
Sliced it down the seams
Dizzy Dizzy
You must be busy
Taking care of Less
Because more is More
Of Me, a Roar.
I still know Who's best.

Tantrika

The art of Tantra
is achieving enlightenment
By means
Of
Ecstasy

By means of
Orgasm

So
Let me
Heal
You

Move through you
Balance your chakras
attune you
to the Universe

allow you to
take
Space
In my healing womb

You are safe here

I can carry
your wounds
the guttural release
of your every trauma

detach you from this world
You
are Safe in me

Surrender yourself
for this moment
of pure Light

Bring me your burdens
I dissolve them in breath

I promise no harm to you.

Surrender. Be Held.

I promise you
everything.

You can just

Let
Go.

Open letter to a little black girl

It's harder than you think
But the Universe
Will give you
Every answer
When you're ready to hear it

You may not believe this, but you have everything you need
already.

One day you'll read this and hear yourself
Your art
Your work touching someone else's hands
Someone reading your truth

Shake the world
In your truth

You are the answer to all of your questions
You have eyes that see each opportunity
You are the medium
And the ending

If not for you
I wouldn't be here
I wouldn't
Edit
Or cry
Or scream about
What I think should be

Perfect.

You are that. You are perfect. You have a Knowing. A Love. A
Boundless creation
Of energy and Light.

Bask in that glow, bitch.
You deserve nothing short of the best.

This world
And all the ones in-between

are Yours.

Conjure

Twist me
I'm lost
Cavernous
And reeling
Forget the floor
Know the Names
Repeat them under air

This is home for me

My skin is too tight
Wrangling a soul inside
To funnel
The meats of Unresolved

Move

As if callouses can condition
The rubbing
Of
New wordless states

I am twice
God must be confused

Again

He made me
More
A better special
With yellowed angles

I'm not even here

I'm everywhere
I am you
Reading
This

Look up

So are they

Be lost.
Twisted
Omnipresent
The floor is never right
So leave it
It doesn't deserve
Your wrangled soul

Know your name

Forget skin to know Free
Deprive of light to know Feel

Pitch yourself black
Cavernous
Lost
Twist unseen

Welcome
home.

There's always more.

Saints Place

I sit in holy places
where
my prayer leaps farther
than the ceiling fan
and my soul touches my soles
so I am lifted
off the grounds of judgment

I ponder here
what many have spoken to life
and what more has been whispered
to Ears that listened
and Eyes that believe

even when swayed by sight

there is love
in here

when the doors have opened
and closed
with empty pews spotted with hymnals
I have hummed under the hours
taken by 'same stuff & different days'

there is hope
in here

for I've made the aisle
loitered in the pulpit
and slept through service

for the heart is treasured ground
and the body treads softly
and the voice sings muffled dreams
in the acoustics of consciousness

there is love in here

and when we believe it-
our prayers
never
have far to go.

Coming into Union

I felt
a separate heartbeat
behind my own

He's close

made his way
under my mind
shifted into my skin

controlled me
Made me
Make
Love

Made me
sing
      sway
against the
fogged shower door

And I came

alive.

Meant to Explain it to Him

Today is
        the first day

I did exactly Everything I wanted.

It
took   me
    to a new
            dimension.

Freedom.

Alignment with the Universe

Feels as Oneness

        tracing channels

to the Sky.

Meditation

I've died 1,346 times.

Walked out of this body
Boundless
onto warm space
whispered through the Ether
To see myself
Seeing
What I've already seen

Touched sound.

Grew.

Shrank to nothing.

Allowed Air to kiss my shoulders
Propagated into vibration
Expanded
across
 autumns new sky

Then came
Back

Stealing the breath of quiet afternoons

I came back
Here

To live
To walk
bound in this body

Just to die
"One" more time...

The Witching Hour

I knew she
Would figure me out

The lights flickered
On
    Again

"all by themselves"

The bathroom illuminated
At 3:33am

And
I pretended to sleep

    Knowing

Eventually she'll put all
the pieces
      together.

One Foot In

I'm here for the mystical
The dreams between our reality
The space that aches
Curling
Time
In Jupiter's belly

I am here for the yesterday
And each tomorrow I saw
Before the rest
Of the resting world

I am here
And
   There
And
Home
     in The In-Between

Where Does She Go?

I stood in
My
Own
Memory.

In a house
I've come to know
from Somewhere Else.

I existed
Twice
at Once

This.

Let Me Talk To The Boy

I've been pounding my fist
On the table
About the Boy.

I have prey.

He's just like me.

But he doesn't know
Who he is

To

Know how alike we are

He's been hurt.
Truly Hurt.
The kind that you feel
In the back of your ears
When you hold your sobbing eyes up.

That.

I know that.

its truth
and sadness
mixed
    with a tinge of hopelessness.

You have hurt like I have hurt.

                    Not everyone knows
That
     About
Us.

But I know you
Just as I know myself
You are Me
I am in your Mirror

It all feels like a mirror

Well, he is.

                    We lift the same.

              We even fuck the same kind of girls.

Why don't you
     love me by Now?

You're wasting time in
A career you don't want
With a girl you barely like

Why?

We have looped galaxies
126 times
    together
before

You don't always choose me
   in the End,
             but you always dabble.

See? Saved you time on your Pleaides research.

I know us
   better than you

         the air is sweet in Colorado

I know you
        I am a Poe fan myself

I know you
        Your Mother's eyes are endless

Isn't it time
You know something
    about me?

Climb the Rope. Don't Look Down

My mind grew feet
Grunted
Awake

Rolled through the sheets
Folded
In
Peace

Raised over pillows
Slinked
To the floor

Sat up
Bewildered
From a different yesterday

Pulsed
Forward
from God's Touch

then faded
Back to Life

Can I write you hippie shit?

Peace and Love from the Third Eye Space
There's flowers in here
Filling the room with warm orange
cashmere
Love deep and folly
Be bended into
        NextTime
Speak around the words
They took up too much space
And now we have a Sky
That's purple and excellent
Jarring in Cardinals
        I
Have sex with wind
Be comfort in fresh fall leaves
Hurry my circles in Time
Press velvet into starlight
And coil galaxies unknown
Be Time's trapper
Hasty ropes and iron sides
Be a message Home
Push color over the next edge
Comfort is despised
Print my yes it's a no
Love the backwards
Keep toes high
Sprinkles rice cake
Apple but
        Hold the sexy.
                Bi.

I Gotchu

I let you fill the room
Shape
Our air into
new presence

forget
what meeting
Is supposed to feel like.

I'll tend to you

Weight
    Less.

He Always Calls (Slam)

I'm not answering the phone anymore. The rattling ring of truly unconcerned call to tell of their boyfriend that has ruined their lives I'm sure wont matter two weeks from today. And even though their screaming rant on the other end has always kept my attention, tonight it's a missed call.

He always calls,
Randomly
And yet systematically tears every bit of faithfulness out of me
To the point where I have to hang up to keep some sense of esteem.
All to myself.
I used to listen to Him
And on Sunday mornings
He and I would come to an agreement
To better this soul of mine through discipleship and servitude
And when long days dragged me into nothing more than a crying heap
Of raging and stressed hormones and forty-five pound textbooks
He'd call
And we'd talk
And I'd listen

But one day long passed
I stopped answering
I stopped listening to the truth He said
And started making up my own lies and my own life to follow.
I missed the call one day
And then the next
And then the next

And then the next
And when the going got tough I called out to him
I tried, and I tried, again, and again.
No answer came.
So I screamed and damn near killed for help no one but...
No one but He could save me.
And I begged, and I asked for forgiveness
For punishment
For all the bullshit
And the scars that I know I have gashed onto peoples hearts
And when I opened my mouth, this mouth
With its malevolent tongue that has sealed my destiny to being
hell-bound
The only thing that came out was "Why?"

Why live? Why wake up and live this lie? Why keep going and
have to plan the rest of my life? Why am I always in this rush
to slow down? Why me? Why do I feel alone when there are
so many around me? Why does my significant other never
know the truth? Why does my family hate me? Why am I not
trusted? Why do I not have compassion anymore? Why haven't
I seen the "Footprints"? Why am I so violent, so unbecoming,
so self-neglecting? Why have I let my foolish pride run me for
so long? Why have I toyed with the emotions of others for my
own satisfaction? Why have I not come to realize the error of my
ways? Why, God, why?

And all was still.
I sat, and I cried.
Until every ounce of my being shook with dehydration.
All the pain, all the doubt of the living humbled at His feet.
All the angst, the lies
Unleashed the eyes of the Nile that gulfed my bedside.

And after this long wait,
I lifted my head
And I lifted my hands
And I closed my eyes
And for the first time my soul did breathe.

He sent me a text.
The text
This leather-bound book of righteousness
Engraved with golden letters that, no matter how old the
binding, would ever rub away.
And as I turned the flimsy pages with my perspiring palms
I came to stopping point
And rededicated my life to Christ through benediction.

Now unto him who is able to keep you from falling. To present
you faultless before the presence of his glory. To the only wise
God, our saviour, be both majesty, honor, dominion, and power.
Both now and forever. Amen.

Listen.
He always calls.

My Past Life As A Sugar Kingpin

I mixed and fixed their quarters
They don't live with me
They writhe in tired presence
They watch Her Majesty

She tells them daylong shucking
The tenders of the bay
The hemp ropes and missed folly
The coins gain of the day

My sugar is purest air
My fields
In lush
In blood

Are littered with their dreams
Of killing she above
Plantation is my kingdom
They work their hands til raw

Because the night will come

And they will take me all.

I
disrobe and walk the path
know sweet night moist in soil
they pull her from my body
they pass the Spirits coiled

and my nakedness means human,
a human
overthrown
I mixed, unfixed their quarters

And here I die alone.

My Friends

My words clanked
Pink greased
Steel brackets
Sounds cracked the sky
Clatter of silk
Kinetic step
We spread
Disseminate
Clash

Listen to me

Pressured temples
Crumble
Sprinkle each weather
Until we make sense.

There's the round of us
The safe of key
The morning quiet
That's safer than the rest of the day

Dew collects

We see growth spring leaves
We feel sun on our backs
Our skin
Is supple in exposure

Bathe the day
Rest the afternoon
Show me your wrongs
Let me find them and make friends

My words are your friend
My words are for friends
I think you're weirder than me

And that's really hard to be.

I hope you like me, too.
Can we be friends? I'm an adult. I have to
learn how to make friends again.

The Sign You Were Praying For, Sweetie.

I need you Full
     Tireless

Awake.

I owe you my heart
its love is
Omnipotent
just as His

We
    Are
Art
understood
in the eyes
of a broken child

We are
     You are
I am.

Pray On Me

I'm starting to remember
The jubilent
Rattle of chicken bones
Shaking by my fire

The drum and howl
Of a cavernous night

I was the
women?
Of the hour

And the keeper
Of your
Secrets

Mystery
Veiled and valued

Hang on my Word
I won't repeat
These guidances
This warning

I look for you
In the visions I've seen

And I remember
This power
Old hands in multiple
Sheets of time

Touch me.

The healing starts from my womb
To your crisis

Feel anything
But the pain of hate
In the cavernous night

I Know
Your Everything

The messes you carry
Over the sacred threshold
Anointing the face
Oiling the feet

I'm scared for you
But not as scared
As you are

Of me.

Choo-Choo

I bet you lost your train of thought,
Funny, he came over here,
that Train.

I bet you lost your train of thought,
Funny,
        She Came
           Over Here,

That Train.

The Heal

I split sides
    In worry
of how you might find me
    I dove
recklessly
into my own healing

the beauty of dissolving pain carried
is realizing
how much pain
is not even your own

I
hold space
    for growth
cradle your
emotional infancy

know
stepping out of
my
own way
witness fright
of omnipresence
    writhe
at the thought of
      True Endlessness.

I am you and We
and All of Us.

Come find me

between unexplainable possibilities
and
perfect coincidences

Astral

my Soul
stood beside Me
watched me dream

left for Thailand
    slept in the jungle again

walked to the roof

                        dove
                         off

  flew

remembered the thrill of Air

      spun
      weightless

this is Freedom

      Knowing

we can always

      separate

knowing

the Cord brings us back
    together.

Open

My brain

tranced heaven

    backwards

and I never

melted   into   yesterday

like
    that?

Taste Orange

You spread your eyes
so
     I'll fuck your mind.

       I'm in your head.

You're
    not crazy.

for the 1000th time you've asked yourself.

I can
    hear
you

Telepathy tastes orange
perspiring palm
finger down the spine

No, I didn't forget
       that
Either.

           yes, that really happened.

I can
    Hear
you

Yes, I know. Me too.

    out Here

Clear as day.

MindFuck

Poetry
    Is
my brain having
    a word orgasm.

It's a whole mess, these pages

My Moment

Everything

About
    My Moment

is right.

      Touch Power.

Let it grace you.
Tranquility and euphoria.

I break under these letters.

you know
Us.

The "mmmmhhmmm"

The breeze off the ocean at 88 degrees.

My subconscious mind tickled yours.

you were
of thirst

an aching

and I took

      You

to my
Somewhere Else.

that's the power
that's the riddle
that's the question you
         Forgot

to ask.

showing your mind
a blindness

a new color
        of
forever

deciding
to see
        every hue known

you.
        bend.
reality.

That is the chase.

your brain takes a step
        Too far
the ledge you fell from
doesn't exist as it existed
the Somewhere Else
Is magic
        danger
the Beyond Now
is truth
        raw
            ground
            Out

from The Ego
        flushed to Soul
to a place with no numbers
feeling
chances

the body is entranced
        organs
caress themselves from the
Outside
In

essence is carbonized

space is more
        Space
the expanse
its circular freedom
the come
d
    o
    w
n
Makes this (Real)ity finite

the Truth
is
    molecularly
bigger than Sky.

limit limitlessness
where time is
        suspended
as liquid motion
the halt
of unstoppable
perfects,
        folds us Open
hoping
we make bliss
        malleable
watching
        the vibrant color
    Of
Forever
    change
again.

"I Don't Know What It Is About Her"

I looked just like
someone you
    knew

someone you used to know

sound just like
something you used to

like
    about someone else

we traded futures

I just woke up
In this one
    again

"What do you mean gifted?"

Am I psychic
Or is
    this
psychosis?

    shouldn't I already know?

my brain spreads flat
bleeding over edge of page

    to

forget
what's Known

or is
    this
     hypnosis?

nowhere for Going to go

dripping Mind as genius rage

Deteriorating Gist

and time raged on
flying past the arcs of memory
 up
to clouds that have been parted for me
yet I watched it fly
whip lashing the phenomena
In-between
dropping minutes of mayhem

and time raged on
leaving my Earth
To the wreckage of ticking
busted the eardrums
of those lost to weeks, months, decades
years attached to the ages
thickening our skin
thinning our souls
funneling us down
cones of a rethought existence

and time raged on
the scattering shards of our plates
sliced those left breathing
left standing
wondering
splitting our air in the matrix we created
confronting the continuum
Of ceaselessness
resting pieces of clarity
upon the deteriorating gist
of everything
pulling beneath the ropes we walk daily
and we could not cry
and we could not dream
and we could not see
and we could not think
and we could not be
what Time wanted us to be
    we could not end
        we did not believe

time raged on

Toss yourself
so madly
into your work
    you can't
help
     but
heal
through
   Creation.

"Zoo Space/Space Zoo"

I prowled this watering hole.

learned to drink the Moon
sipped stars to backbone
loved the other sides of Dark
flipped forests
ate pieces we don't talk about

Let's talk

I spun magick
that's the glory of spinning
My tail tripped Time in its whirling
creased and pressed
backed reality into humid corners
the Handing Over
over handing
of what I have always known
stirring in
marrows
and mood rings that actually

Work

I worked tirelessly
to cup your ears
From my volume
of our Truth

She's loud

She roars and shatters
Pierced glass air
To grain
Bounced
      Off
electricity
      Boing
against
    Your Universe
              Make noise with me.

Prey. Clatter. Shock. Pace.

I'm from Space
      I am Space
Delicious unknown
    Purring
in Saturn's back pocket.

"Can you see the End of the World?"

Famine across the pond
Will grow the world tired

We will simply run out of things we Need.

The people will realize the government has
nickeled and dimed us
into our own oblivion
until the Poor cannot afford to breath 'cleaned' air.

We are paying for our own End
We eat more than we make. We waste with no more space for
waste.
We don't have enough room to make more artificial
environments

When the bees are gone,   that's it.
All the psychics are seeing the same thing.

Now you should be worried.

the awakened many will march the White House
in black clothes
        black masks
with red cheeks and loud voices

we will tread to tyranny
bash
thrones
we helped them make

The world will physically   tilt
our vibrations
will make new space

and those of us
unwilling to Change
for the sake Humanity

Will stay put on this dying Earth

the Rest
the gleaming rest
will transcend the planet
start Anew
    with Society
of no time and no money
sustained in pressurized galaxy.

Clairvoyant

I speak his thoughts past yesterday's oblivion
so we could have been spoken tomorrows
on the Others side

resting repose
in the mediums of betrayals
in the rituals of the unseen
in the debts of the shadow

we bargained souls
who unhanded their troubles
in the midst of eternity
and
nights clammer (h)our composure
debouching our day
synchronizing the supernatural
with the quartz gem
of timelessness

how must I live?
how must they not?
or is passage the pathway
to
some thing
more than time
and less than human?

By Him
sleep has Covered the worthless...

but I
am an insomniac.

Trippy Logic

Time has color
Sound makes
seconds prisms

So they call
And they call

and I just know the answers.

and they piece
and they puzzle

missing details they brushed off
too many times

and they wake
wonder
how many questions can
     she answer

to make me feel
as the person I am supposed to be

and they pray
and they wait

 And they Settled
they settle
little mysteries
that cannot be explained
on their own.

 That's the phone ringing

That's the Knowing

Would you always
 want to know
 Why?

Breach

    realized
air purple

march
messy thoughts
over color

spatter the experience
of tribe
in the night

the visits of Me
Loop Karmic ties
Move.
    Fit me.
I sing their voices.

in Spirit Dance

I hear the call
ladling
Earth and Sound

in the suck
of a breached existence.

The Love Story

Let hearts touch Night
We are
        unyielding purple
flecks of imagining
I don't
have a name for

Us.

nothing was right for the both of us
when we met and fell in love
that's the fun part
we are Seuss salad
burning memories

The time it takes to grow the fuck up
Is all the time we need

Spirit has a wind
if you
silence the mind
the vibration of everything we know
reaches out to touch you

you cannot pretend
once you know

the illusionist is all of us.

cranking machines we
did not know we built
song and dance
of lives that never truly end

we loop
        back.

we make contracts
with souls
shed skins
of our parents' hurt
ancestral pain
Our tribes' tears

connected
the stars have shown us
for ages
How to live and die
and return
to live and die
and return again

meet me in the matrix
I am here
tinkering with time

She's
 not
even
    linear.

"Tell Me Some Psychic Shit"

You've made a list
of problems about

yourself

and seem to believe they are truth.

your ego   lies
     runs
fears potential

You are everything you need.

Your creative space should be preserved
just as the vats
just as the vineyard

You listen to your Self.
he's starving for the deepest real you have.

the begging
the harp
and helplessness

met you in my song somewhere

and I sing you
over
and
over

we syncopate
Until the octave travels us clean

let's be the Freaks
And be ok with that.

I have nothing
but ears for your depth

I love you

    Fuck.

I wasn't ready to say that right now
but it's the truth

but I've made a list of problems
about myself
I have convinced myself are
true.

you know me.

    Know

You already wrote this Into me.

The price of him

He has a price

I cost him
his ego

I cost him friends.

His life of glass will shatter.

but a love
unconditional
is too brave
         too raw
for money alone.

you are
priceless
to me

you saved my life
and
you didn't even know

you held me
in suspense
long enough
to
leave
        Her.

long enough to see what was
               wrong.

and
I broke

I spilled over the counter
across the kitchen floor

but you shined in
with no pause

Swept me up
barefoot

forced me on
one
more
day

as someone to see soon
"Something to look forward to"

I found
Something
to look forward to

I found someone
to look forward to

and it pressed me
passed the days
of gray
and snow

I shattered
        Knowing
you would
make us
a mosaic.

I
shattered
        Knowing
the pricelessness
of
our He(art)

Over Under Think

Did you guess me?
I am a brainteaser

a living
breathing
feather in your cerebellum

here
festering for your attention

it's my job to orange

       See?

Like that.

I was taken by heart
Into
Bliss.

I touched God.

Filled my body with Crystal
Alkalized
To a new realm

This isn't my only reality.

I'm someone new

Healed.
Purified.

Released to the new worlds freedom

There's more for us out there
There's
More
        Than
This.

Be still to know.
Stay still to partake.

Hex Code #RRGGBB

It took us centuries
to draw grey lines in our sky
meet like wind
curled and whipping
fresh reality
into the unpackaged day

we can forget
tuck
the perfect coincidence
in shallow pockets

walking
grey lines
to sky absent
Our
colors

Day 4: When I Post Send Prayers

My
Grandmother
whispered "Get up, baby girl.'

I know I don't smell good
I did not leave the bed

I haven't left my house in three days.

I laid
    In Our Bed
cried
for three days

    grieved the loss of my marriage.

This
    Is
The

Darkest Night of My Soul.

all the words

                I have strength to say.

"What does it feel like?"

Remembering
    a memory
you never had

feeling the memory
in your body
as
    you
watch
    a show
of Everyone Else's story

Maybe I am too

close

to the sky up
   here

maybe this Other Door
swings as half saloon doors in Westerns

it's the Wild West up
   here.

there's a naked Man walking around my apartment

a Spirit crossing
       Over

deciding

     to Go

    maybe I am sitting alone too long. Her deployment is long.

we

made eye contact

don't sit

on my couch

I don't like naked bodies on my couch

     Its suede

I am never sure what they are looking for.
they are always surprised when I say hello

as if they didn't have phones in their lifetime.

Well.

I guess this is different.

one day you existed
   and then you didn't.
to go back to existing again to someone
   must be
strange.

      its makes me feel like death is a joke.

we never really go.

we just take our Higher Self

to a more equipped body
There's More To All Of Us

       Perv. Get out of the bathroom
I have to go
and I don't know if you can see me or not

I'm tiptoeing around you? In MY apartment.
How funny.

              I laughed at sage.
I really did.

until I smudged my house
and they
    all ran past my wrists

so

its just you today

"hello.
"what are you looking for?"

Doc Martens Or Nothing

You can call me
a fast lifer
whatever you see
but
in a past living

                              I was a rockstar

gluttonous and dazzling
shirring insecurities
and a perfect face to hide every single one
endless eyes that shimmer
over eager arms
spanning out the scuffed stage.

performer
        and fan.

The Purple Robot Alien Emoji

If I told you I was an alien, you'd freak.
so instead I'll say

the future is smooth
burnished
breathless
    unforgettable

Cerulean.
the best blue there is.

and you can
is
and
Be
and
    Been

All at once.

your rigid bones
bend
better
 There

We cheat your 3D.
Cymatics
Free will and "feelings"

because everything is vibration.

It
really really
    is.

The Letter To The Youth I'm
Not Allowed To Send.

I encourage your creative
now is the time to set your Soul afire
Do drugs.
Have slutty sex.
Make Life The Bitch You Own.

"They" don't matter.
all of "this" is not even real.
when you realize you're part of God's imaginarium
you will start to live a life worth living.

Know Goodness.
She's euphoria rolled in moons
of ecstasy

Find Music again.

Do that.
Feel that.

Break your mind

Again

then put it back together as it should be

Lose yourself in your craft.

focus makes craze
deraged makes Happy.
Force fury through your eyes

Cry tears of Creation.

   Touch everything.

Touch the You

Hold You Close
No one has in a long time

Heal yourself.
Heal your Time

Love Yourself
so deeply
there's no room for sadness

anymore

And The Rest will fall into Place.

Clearing

Heal me.
I walked alone.

I waited at school by myself one more time until some staff took me home. Feeling forgotten hurts. Feeling like there is no one to fall on hurts. Getting up by myself hurts, knowing if I didn't no one would help anyways. Accept the fact that there were times she didn't care. Accept the fact that people change, but assume the damage done leaves with their old habits. You do not need to feel anxious anymore. No one is coming after you. You are safe in your skin. You have completeness if you choose. Heal me. I saw your face after the stroke and I knew you were still in there. I know your eyes. I know what your eyes mean when they look at me. No stroke can change that. I miss you. You didn't mean to leave, but you left. And so did Papa. And so did Walt. And so did Pop. And Sean. And Wes. And Gary. And Gram. And they still look at us. They watch us from above with suggestions and smiles. They don't like any of our music choices. Heal me. She's still in love with her ex. Her ex is still in love with her, but she is on baby 26 and they are all beautiful. My ex finally recovered from addiction. If you ever read this I am proud of you, but that is all I want to say. They will need another exorcism. I thank God for this even though I blocked you. Heal me. I was a really good wife. I ironed your shit in the morning, and had dinner cooked on the table by 5. I still want to be a wife one day again. One day soon. Heal me. You threw away my clothes when you did not like them, and I will hate you for that for a really long time. I know every time you went through my phone. I know you followed me to work one day, just to see if that was where I was really going. I never said I saw you.

Just because I don't say anything doesn't mean I don't know. Silence has served me well. But this is my voice. She heals me. Heal me. You don't have to like me, you just have to respect my choices. They aren't yours. I am not you. Heal me. You watch too much porn. It disconnects us, poisons our mind away from The Human Condition. Poisoned like our water and meats. Heal me. My client followed me home, sent people to my door. I almost stopped working in this field for that. Heal me. She's jealous and she should not be. We come from the same place, same womb. I miss the best friend my sister was. Heal me. I am insecure. Heal me. I still get nervous teaching. Heal me. Am I old enough to be sexy? Heal me. I have enough money this time to do things. Heal me. My writing is good enough. Heal me.

My writing is good enough
Heal me
My writing is good enough
Heal me
My writing is good enough
Heal me
My voice is good enough
Heal me

                              All of me is good enough.
                     Healed.

Hello.
This is Alisha's ego.
I'm here bitch, fuck a title.
sharp-tongued
brutally honest,
and
        purposefully so
she hates you coy
This is who "Needs to leave"
I know I need to get off of me
but she cannot get rid of me

She, fuck I
Like that shit

I like when you look twice

I like that I am on your mind

I like that I know
that I do
what I want
because
I just didn't care
in the moment

It felt good.

I just care about me.

Because
　　　I have righteous anger
I can furrow into flirting
And perfect skin
And perfect hips
And perfect lips

And eyes, bitch. Eyes for fucking days.

I serve you these eyes once, and you're gone.

I'm bigger than you. My pussy is better than yours.

I can scoop you
And your bitch, bitch.

And never need to return a favor.

I bounce off silence
I walked In. Admire me

I turn heads. I know how sexy I am. I like to pretend that I don't
to see if I drive you crazy.

　　　Ol lookin' ass motherfucker

I reject you
and you
and you
and you

I am sick, I know.
Yes, I'm this pretty in 'real life'
That ass is fat baby, I know.
She works for it, ask her her max.

You never had a chance.

Yes, I work out. Tell me more.
I know what I'm doing
      to you

See, me, Ego
I cannot let her go just yet
She needs me

Lately I've been holding on tighter
I don't wanna say some weak shit
But
Fuck.
        I'm dying

I don't know what this bitch did but now I am dying.

you better not
don't you open your fuckin' mouth about it

She needs me, alright?

I'm just the kinda shitty person she needed for awhile
To protect her Soul. And I like it here.

I get to say all the mean things people think I would think.

But now her Soul is all huge and whatnot. *Whatever.*
she needed me
she really really did

To be safe from the world
instead of being the Alisha that she
is
when she is
    actually Happy.

I am hard to shake.
I sit and cross my legs because I know you're already looking

I'm handsy
I'll grab it

Because you'll never tell Me no.
They never do.

Shit. I'm ugly
Shit. We're ugly
I can't be Ugly

Is this part of me?

                                        Don't publish Alisha,

    I'll die.

"What is Enlightenment?"

2016 is when I
　　Knew today.

and I Heal Me.

that love
transcends
　　permeates

all the parts that make you uncomfortable

about
You.

And I Heal You.

And I throw the sun

　　In the Sky

each morning for you

　　　　to be happy.

I can't be anyone's happy

until
　　I am.

because we are of a making
of the Most High.

leave your religion
for the Gospel.

happiness is every yes of a moment.

a gentle Divine.
a finding of Self in Twelve Dimensions.

    Bliss.

I touched it and it shook my every cell into chocolate.

    Yes.

It's the Everything of All you can ever Feel.

    Eternal Love.

I will
     never
be
    the Same.

The Closing

You might think I've lost my mind
I did
    for a second
But that
      second was
Genius

to fill
These pages
    3,682,407 times
      again.

To You, the reader:

Stay irate. Close the back door only when you need. Feed the
forest your pleasing. Take space, salvage the Saturn and silly,
fester a God awake. Here are our dwellings. Master the fury of
routine then rip it down the middle. You Create the Now and
all of its buffoonery. Wiggle your heart, a broken peace jangles
in needy pockets. Open treasure. The marks of You are seven
holes and 12 chakras. Forget your name. Fall steadfast into
healing and be the You behind your Name. Your headstone
is warming. You need death to remind you to live. Be ancient
with me. Show me touch, tremor, tyranny. Hate something, feel
eviscerated. Draw new lines in quicksand. Toy with words and
love the Truth of you. This is The Happy. The Knowing of More
and the Bringing of You to Yourself. Be prepared to wade, and
bother like a mustard stain on the 4th of July.

Stay hot like Nikky Finney.

Stay hot like you. You don't need big words to sound like you know what you are doing.

Go be Everything.

That's the
Magick
    Of
You.

The Riddle

This is the poem where I bear my Soul
And give you a Mindfuck

She's a beautiful soul
with
   so
    much
    hurt
blinking is a blessing in the morning for my tears.

my biggest fear is being scared of being small.

I never want to cower in a corner again.

I never want to quiet in question.

I'm fucking lonely
    A Lot.

And I don't give a shit what it looks like

I'm fucking me.

    Some days I barely breathe in this body

these good genes save me

and I hurt for that.

I want you
       to know me
              the real me

that gets tired
       the one that is an open scar sometimes.

when you realize I'm a real person

with a broken heart
with a dozen problems you would never guess
I
would
       ever
have.

Who Ever Are We?

       Why waste more time telling you what to See.

It's like climbing over a fence that isn't even there.

I love you.
and that's the Truth.

I love each and every one of you.
I don't sleep. I pray for you.

but I have to love Me
and
I didn't for a really long time.

and days got long
and
then one day I forgot everything
and then
remembered all of The Problems and how they came to be

and it made me realize that my other biggest fear is loving
someone who can't truly love me back as I do.

Catharsis.

So….

I muddy my heart to sky
For
    You….
       when I find You

To the One who I am looking for

I'd give….
       There's nothing else to Give

But

Love,
    That's
        All
I am.

That's all I came for, _____.

Love me,
Please?

Im sorry i love you

i don't know what I just felt all over my body but I just realized what my soul feels like

She's a cool ass bitxh OMG

I JUST MET MY OWN SOUL.

Must be friday

HOLY FUCKING SHIT

"and they gave no fucks and lived happily ever…after?"

Acquainted is an untamed collection of poetry and prose about our deepest truths, trauma, love, sex, and spiritual awakening. The book is divided into four chapters, each chapter sharing a facet of the journey to self-realization. Share our life with The Others. Open our hearts to the Lovers. Come clean about The Rest. Try to solve The Riddle. Acquainted is the ugly, honest conversation we all need to have to know and honor our truest self.

About the Author

Alisha Chelsea Jones is a social worker, yoga teacher, and poet living in Washington, DC with way too many houseplants. Her love for writing and dance began in the A.R.M.E.S afterschool program at The Fine Arts Center in Greenville, SC as a means of therapy and has blossomed into a lifestyle blog, slam performance, and individually published works in adulthood. Alisha's charismatic personality shines through her writing as she tells our stories of self-love, positivity, and being unapologetically vulnerable to heal.

CPSIA information can be obtained
at www.ICGtesting.com
Printed in the USA
FSHW021412101219
64689FS